Mental Power

Orison Swett Marden

Kessinger Publishing's Rare Reprints

Thousands of Scarce and Hard-to-Find Books
on These and other Subjects!

- Americana
- Ancient Mysteries
- Animals
- Anthropology
- Architecture
- Arts
- Astrology
- Bibliographies
- Biographies & Memoirs
- Body, Mind & Spirit
- Business & Investing
- Children & Young Adult
- Collectibles
- Comparative Religions
- Crafts & Hobbies
- Earth Sciences
- Education
- Ephemera
- Fiction
- Folklore
- Geography
- Health & Diet
- History
- Hobbies & Leisure
- Humor
- Illustrated Books
- Language & Culture
- Law
- Life Sciences
- Literature
- Medicine & Pharmacy
- Metaphysical
- Music
- Mystery & Crime
- Mythology
- Natural History
- Outdoor & Nature
- Philosophy
- Poetry
- Political Science
- Science
- Psychiatry & Psychology
- Reference
- Religion & Spiritualism
- Rhetoric
- Sacred Books
- Science Fiction
- Science & Technology
- Self-Help
- Social Sciences
- Symbolism
- Theatre & Drama
- Theology
- Travel & Explorations
- War & Military
- Women
- Yoga
- *Plus Much More!*

We kindly invite you to view our catalog list at:
http://www.kessinger.net

IX. MENTAL POWER

THE development of mental power affords the best investment for a youth's capital, — his time and energy. It pays to discipline one's mind so as to discover what one can do best, and to form the mental habits which underlie success in life.

It does not pay to study Latin only a few weeks, "in order to get an insight into it;" to learn French in twelve lessons, if "the master will not plague the pupil with verbs and participles;" or to educate the family on the cooperative plan, "by a subdivision of Rome, the mother in picture galleries, the daughter at the monuments, and the father studying local color in the cafés."

We live in an age of haste. Some people seem to look at an egg, like the Chinese sage, "and expect to hear it crow." It is an era of "universities," "colleges," "professors," — with "short courses" that lead no one knows whither. We behold around us educated men of an earlier generation who believed with Josh Billings that it is better not to know so many things than to know so much that is not so.

We rejoice in "university extension." It creates an atmosphere favorable for study and awakens the intellectual power of isolated pupils; yet the cramming of people's heads with facts leaves them uneducated, unless, in some other way, the power of original thinking is developed and the mind made ready to act upon the instant.

Education is mind-training for power. It is not only to sharpen one's tools, but also to make him who handles the tools more of a man.

"An education is no phonograph," says President Barrows, "to repeat mechanically what is poured into it, but a dynamo for the generation of power, for the illumination, movement, and gracious-handed comfort of mankind."

It is this kind of knowledge that enters into the mental bone and blood, so to speak, and it is the best paying investment. With our vast educational plant in America, expending four hundred million dollars a year, mind-training is power practically within every one's reach.

Yet with nearly seventeen million pupils in our public schools, very few advance beyond the highest grammar grade; and, as long as this is so, mind-training for power is the lot of the few, not of the many. Certainly it cannot be said concerning those that do not study in the higher grades that they are educated in the sense in which Plato understood it, — having that discipline "which gives to the body and to the soul all the beauty and all the perfection of which they are capable."

To make the most possible of one's self — discovering, developing his own powers, learning to use them to promote his own ends and the good of mankind — is the true purpose of man's education. It is the unfolding of nature, — of all that nature has given to him. To learn to think, to love the objects that ought to be loved, to direct the will to right ends, to observe, to reason, to exercise sound judgment, to control self, and to influence others, require time and teachers.

Nature does not make a specialist, a mere memory-gland or a money-gland, but her aim is a full-orbed man. If we develop the body exclusively, man deteriorates toward the brute. If we press all the vital energies of life into muscle-making we dwarf the soul and tear down manhood. It is an inexorable law of nature that what is exercised in one's daily vocation or as a special discipline becomes stronger. It was nature's intention that our faculties should be exercised in a healthy, symmetrical manner. Any other course creates one-sidedness and discord. Cultivate the higher faculties of the brain alone, and expend all life's energies in expanding the power of the intellect, and what do we get? Not a full-orbed, well-rounded philosophy, but a cold, unsympathetic, one-sided mentality, devoid of all the finer graces, the warmer sympathies, the more delicate sentiments. Develop the moral nature alone, or even the spiritual, without the mental and the physical, and we have a fanatic, a zealot, an unbalanced enthusiast.

The object of a watch is to keep as perfect time as possible. This time is not kept by the medium of any one tiny screw, or lever, or wheel, but is the resultant of the harmonious action of all, and depends upon the perfection of the minutest portion of the watch. So the object of all education and culture is the symmetrical development of all the legitimate faculties and functions.

" Perhaps the most valuable result of all

education," said Huxley, "is the ability to make yourself do the thing you have to do when it ought to be done, whether you like it or not; it is the first lesson which ought to be learned, and, however early a man's training begins, it is probably the last lesson he learns thoroughly." Conformity to order, courage, and decision of character, and formation of the habits of industry, regularity, punctuality, thoroughness, persistency, patience, self-denial, intelligence in citizenship, and a wholesome self-respect, are characteristic of mind-training for power.

The practical working of a long course of schooling is thus shown by Professor Holden of the Lick Observatory in a quotation from a paper prepared by him on education at West Point:

"There is absolutely no favoritism in the treatment of the students by their instructors. Every academic performance is rated by a simple and effective marking-system, which is an essential part of the method of the school. Absolute and complete justice is attained more nearly than in any other organization which it has been my fortune to study. I have never heard it seriously questioned by any student, officer, or professor. The work of each cadet is therefore thoroughly tested every day, and no failure can possibly be hidden. The effect on the character of a student is immediate and admirable. He learns in the recitation-room, as everywhere else, not to shirk his duty; and he learns what few in civil life learn so early, that every short-coming in the course of duty is sure to bring its corresponding penalty. High class-standing makes subsequent promotion in the army quick and certain. There is no moment when a cadet does not fully understand that his performance of duty now will influence his whole official career. This is fully recognized, and its perfect justice is admitted by all. The effect of diligence and faithfulness in the performance of allotted tasks is perfectly understood, and consequences follow actions with certainty. Every official delinquency has its appropriate number of demerit marks. Lateness at roll-call carries one demerit; absence, ten; slight untidiness in dress, one; inattention to duty or at drill, five, and so on.

"No cadet can have more than a certain small total number of demerits (some two hundred in a year) and remain in the academy. If he has more than the allowed total, he is dismissed. If he has fewer, his rank in his class is proportionately lowered, and his over privileges are curtailed, precisely as if he had failed in his studies. For an army officer good official conduct is at least as necessary as a knowledge of chemistry. Every delinquency is reported in writing, and each one involves a written explanation. Failure to render such an explanation is itself a delinquency. If the cadet has no excuse he must say so officially. If he has a sufficient excuse no demerit attaches to the offense. Each cadet must therefore examine his official conscience (so to speak) regularly, and record the results. All ill feeling is avoided, as the whole record is in writing and there are no personal reprimands.

There is no talking. Only simple laws are prescribed. Each one of them is just. Every allowance is made for inexperience. Every reasonable excuse is admitted. The final result is like the result of gravitation, inevitable, inexorable, just, immediate."

West Point training is, in the end, specialized, being military. Other schools of advanced grade test men differently, but the result of the broadest education is mental power. A youth is seized upon, his capacities are discovered, his desire for knowledge is stimulated, and he is taught how to acquire it; the

development of his own ability to go forward
is the end sought, and he is prepared to take
advantage of the boundless possibilities of
life. He is not well educated who is not made
morally better, more trustworthy, sweeter in
spirit, more conscientious and of greater force
in right living. It is this that gives the sense
of a certain solidity of disciplined powers and
that serenity of spirit and self-poise which we
look for in man, who was created in the moral
and spiritual image of his Maker.

It is as much a part of true education to
develop appreciation and love of all forms of
beauty and goodness, wherever found, as it
is to learn grammar and arithmetic. Tolera-
tion, charity, and broad sympathy and love
for our fellow-men are necessary parts of a
true education. The most highly cultured
man is he who has the greatest number of the
highest products of the best mental development in the most refined form. Such a man
is the highest mental expression of humanity.

The only real success worthy of the name
is that which comes from a consciousness of
growing wider, deeper, higher in mental and
moral power as the years go on. To feel the
faculties expanding and unfolding, to feel
the leaven of the truth permeating the whole

being, is the only life worth living. Such a life is neither drudgery nor a dream. It is rather the exquisite result of high qualities finely disciplined.

Many an extraordinary man has been made out of a very ordinary boy; but, in order to accomplish this, we must begin with him while he is young. It is simply astonishing what training will do for a rough, uncouth, and even dull lad if he has good material in him and comes under the tutelage of a skilful educator before his habits have been confirmed. Even a few weeks' or months' drill of the rawest and roughest recruits in the late Civil War so straightened and dignified stooping and uncouth soldiers, and made them so manly, erect, and courteous in their bearing, that their own friends scarcely knew them. If this change is so marked in a youth who has grown to maturity, what a miracle is possible in the lad who is taken early and put under a course of drill and systematic training, both physical, mental, and moral! How many a man who is now in the penitentiary, in the poorhouse, among tramps, or living out a miserable existence in the slums of our cities, bent over, uncouth, rough, slovenly, has possibilities slumbering within his rags which would have developed him into a magnificent man, an ornament to the human race instead of a foul blot and scar, had he only been fortunate enough early in life to have come under efficient and systematic training!

Only four out of a hundred go to high schools, academies, seminaries and business schools, and only one-fourth of these go to college. Yet the colleges are gaining in patronage. William T. Harris, United States Commissioner of Education, states that in each million of people the number of those receiving an education above that of the grammar schools is three times as great as it was twenty-five years ago.

The necessity for earning money at an early age, or a passion for business on the part of young people in thrifty families, keeps many from pursuing longer courses of study. We often hear a father say that it is not necessary for his son to go to college in order to make money; as if mere wealth could be compared with an elevated, expanded, and ever-growing mind; as if money, with a narrow horizon, with a sordid and rutty life, can for a moment compare with the satisfaction which comes from being put into touch with all the world by a mind which has been electrified by a love for knowledge, and which has learned how to acquire it! Is it not the tendency of this age to put the interrogation point of commercial value upon everything? "Will the thing pay?" "What is there in it?" These are the questions too often asked. But what a mean, sordid view of life it is to look upon it as a mere mint for coining money, as if there were nothing higher or nobler for the grandest of God's creation than the piling up of wealth, the accumulating of houses and estates! Are the heart's yearnings, the soul's longings, to be satisfied with the piling up of material possessions?

There is something hardening, demoralizing, in the modern money-making career which tends to destroy all the finer instincts for the good, the beautiful, and the true, which dries up all sympathy for the misfortunes of others, dwarfs the growth of one's higher self, and crushes out the nobler impulses. One of the strangest and most unaccountable things in human experience is the fact that men will struggle and strive, day and night, for years and years, trying to make the most possible out of the farm, the shop, the trade, or the profession, — in other words, to develop their vocation to its utmost, to raise it to its highest point, — and yet utterly neglect the culture of their own higher powers.

The highest character, the noblest manhood, can never be developed under a low, sordid aim; and if a course in a college or a university could do nothing more than elevate the ideals and give a broader and truer outlook upon life, it would be well worth the time spent.

Every youth owes it to himself and to the world to make the most possible out of the stuff that is in him, to develop himself, not partially, not narrowly, nor in a one-sided way, but symmetrically, — in a large way. It is as much his duty to make the largest possible man of himself as it is the function of an acorn to become a grand oak, — not a little sapling, but a mighty tree which stands alone, buffets the storms and tempests, and furnishes shelter for man and beast and timber for the shipbuilders.

"We should so live and labor in our time," said Beecher, "that what came to us as seed may go to the next generation as blossom, and that what came to us as blossom may go to them as fruit."

This is the end of this publication.

Any remaining blank pages are for our book binding
requirements and are blank on purpose.

To search thousands of interesting publications like this one,
please remember to visit our website at:

http://www.kessinger.net

Printed in the USA
CPSIA information can be obtained
at www.ICGtesting.com
LVHW081202071124
795973LV00010B/1838

9 781162 817507